Building **STRONG SOLID** FOUNDATIONS

Author: Beverly Coffee-Vereen

Published by: Gifted Publications
giftedpublications.com

© Copyright 2021 Teach Me Tech, LLC

All rights reserved. No part of this publication may be reproduced, stored in a retrieval system, or transmitted, in any form or by any means, electronic, mechanical, photocopying, recording, or otherwise, without the written prior permission of the author.

Created in the United States of America

Foreword

It has been my pleasure to know Beverly Coffee-Vereen for over a year. Since we met, I have watched her publicly and privately showcase her love for God where her heart burns with the desire to go deeper and deeper in the knowledge of the beauty of the Lord. You can easily tell she is passionate about helping others find Love in God as well.

Chris Cater

Foundations

The Bible speaks of building on solid foundations. Anything worth building has to have a foundation in order to strive, survive, and grow. Some examples of foundations include; marital relationships, friendships, business, and family foundations, to name a few.

The type of foundation that a person lays will surely determine how long something will last. A strong solid foundation will last a lifetime.

These types of foundations will cause you to withstand violent storms, outlast Crises, and take whatever turbulence that approaches your life.

When I was growing up, my mom raised nine children. She would always tell us to stand with the decisions that we made. In other words, remain consistent. She taught us that material possessions do not determine who you are, but character does. Character is how you behave when no one is watching. She would say things like, "Treat others the way you desire to be treated" or "Trouble is easy to get into, but hard to get out of." As I reflect back on some of her teachings or clichés she shared, I realize that she was building strong, solid foundations to help us navigate through life. I still hear her voice at times, building our self-esteem and sometimes being hard on us. She was very overprotective.

The Three Little Pigs

As I think about building foundations, I'm reminded of the story of The Three Little Pigs and how they ventured out on their own. The first two pigs did not build on a strong foundation. They did not take the time or put much effort into their homes. They used flimsy straw and sticks. Therefore when trouble (the wolf) appeared, they were unprepared, and their homes were destroyed. Thank God that the third pig was built on a solid foundation, using brick. The last little pig provided the other two with safety, protection, and survival. Because of that, the pigs were able to escape the wolf. There are so many life lessons in that story. It happens to be one of my favorites.

Women

When women build on strong foundations, they will never compromise to stay in unhealthy relationships or degrade themselves to please others. Also, they will never settle for less when they know their true worth. This depends on how their foundation was built.

Solid foundations will cause one to roll with the punches, as well as move ahead in life. If the base is shaky and weak, then it would be a great time to consider rebuilding. I happen to think rebuilding is good when one comes to the realization that it is time to do so. There is nothing wrong with rebuilding or reconstructing. We all have to do it periodically. Sometimes goals change and situations in life, so we have to continue to work on our foundation as needed. The foundation must support the changes we are encountering.

Men

Now let's look at the men. When a man is presented with a strong foundation early in life, he will be a person that is motivated, determined, and unstoppable! He will learn how to make good decisions, take constructive criticism, and will not run from his responsibilities. A man that has a solid foundation will be ecstatic to advise others how to build sturdy foundations. He will enjoy a stable life, build life-long friendships, and will embrace the challenges that life brings. When he is encompassed with life, he will soar to places unknown. A powerful foundation creates well-rounded fathers and men of wisdom. Would you agree? For both men and women, strong foundations are built deep down inside. These bases will guide them through the valleys and hills of life, leading them to mountaintops. When foundations are laid early in life, it will enhance growth, maturity, responsibility and cause men and women to learn their purpose, guiding them to their destiny. Strong foundations will build resistance.

As I stated earlier, if one realizes that their foundation is rocky or unstable, it is perfectly okay to rebuild. There is nothing wrong with rebuilding.

Just as a house wears out and needs to be repaired or remodeled, it is the same for friendships, relationships, and fellowships. We should never be timid nor procrastinate when it comes to rebuilding. Things will only get worse if we ignore the situation. Not only will matters get worse, but others could also get hurt. If you notice the decay or the rotting of the foundation, rebuild and start over!

Types of Foundations

I agree with the Bible when it says there are two types of foundations: rock or sand. The Bible says a wise man who builds on a rock will overcome and survive various storms. On the other hand, a foolish man will build his foundation on the sand. When the storms of life and trouble come, that man will have a great fall (St. Matthew 7:24).

Let's not be like the foolish man and allow our house to collapse. If this happens, we can only blame ourselves. If we want firm foundations, we simply must build on Jesus, the "Solid Rock." He will carry us through the storms of life, the rain, and the winds that beat vehemently upon us from time to time. Those of you that are reading this book simply must hear His words and take heed like a wise man. Once we decide to do so, we will outlast all of the obstacles that we encounter in life. However, if we do not heed, then we will be deemed as foolish builders. We will have problems surviving life's encounters. Do you know of a person that has been beaten down by life? I am sure you can think of one. Chances are that person did not have a strong foundation. Something was missing.

There is safety in Christ! When we build on the "Solid Rock," we hear his commands and obey his voice.

Let me ask you a few questions. Are you a foolish builder or a wise builder? Are you building on a strong solid foundation in this 21st century? In this life, we shall encounter storms such as rain, strong winds, thunder, lightning, and even a little hail. They will test our foundation to see how strong or solid it really is. These storms will saturate us, blow us down, frighten us, and strike us. All of these disturbances will happen to see if our foundation is sturdy enough or to let us know if we simply need to start over and rebuild.

There are four types of foundations that I would like to elaborate on Spiritual Foundations, Life Foundations, Business Foundations, and Family Foundations. First, let's look at the Spiritual Foundation. A solid spiritual foundation is very necessary for families. This foundation will put us on the right path to finding spiritual identity. A spiritual identity means we will identify with whom and what we believe from a religious perspective. When children are not reared with a spiritual foundation or background, this can cause them to have difficulty identifying with Christ. It can also make it very easy for them to become engaged in various religions that can be confusing.

I wanted to make sure my children could identify with Christ because there will come a time in life when they feel sad, lonely, or perplexed about themselves. A spiritual foundation will help us stay strong in our spiritual walk and understand the will of God for our lives as we progress day-to-day. To help us build spiritually, we must study the bible, give ourselves to sincere prayer, and remain faithful. These tools will help us continue to build our spiritual lives. It is vital to have a strong spiritual foundation in these perilous times that we live in. The bible gives us various scriptures that will help us identify with Christ on a spiritual level. One that comes to mind is St. John 1:12 "Yet to all who did receive him, to those who believed in his name, he gave the right to become children of God." Romans 8:28, Ephesians 1:7, and St. John 15:16 will also help them to identify with Christ. The verses of scripture will speak life and truth to anyone that may be having problems spiritually. It will help us to understand who God created us to be. In my opinion, I feel this should be introduced to young children. It will help them to connect with

God and lead them to a spirit-filled life. It will help people to know that the Lord is their friend, they have been set free, and that we have been redeemed. A solid spiritual foundation will help us both mentally and physically. It's a great feeling to know who you are in Christ and to connect with him!

Next, there are Life Foundations that we must build. These foundations will prepare us for life's issues that cannot be avoided. We will learn how to deal with the ups and downs of life's roller coaster. When life issues arrive, we want to be able to handle them without losing our grip. Having a solid life foundation will strengthen our minds and keep our emotions healthy. A strong life foundation is important.

Then, we also have Business Foundations that must be built. Business foundations will help us become goal-oriented, learn the ins and outs of finances, and how to manage money. All of these structures will help hold us up and keep us strong. If we do not have a solid foundation, we can bend and break down under pressure. Handling business can be stressful in this world. Life has a way of causing us to bend, but we do not want to break. It might be difficult to recover and regain our composure. A great business foundation will put you in a good place to be successful in running your business or running someone else's establishment. That is why it is important to have a firm business foundation.

Finally, I want to mention Family Foundations. All of the foundations are important, but in my opinion, family is the most vital because I believe this is where everything stems from. Our family is whom we grew up with and those that we spent an ample amount of time with. We were born into that family, and these are the people that we mimicked and viewed as role models. It is from aunt's, uncle's, cousin's, and siblings are where we learned and picked up both good and bad habits. Family is where we learn to love and communicate with each other. While I understand that not all families are the same and many are reared differently, however, most families have some resemblance in character as well as features. Strong families show love to each other, celebrate each other's accomplishments, and share their fears, thoughts, and ideas. They stick together through thick and thin, the good and bad. They cover one another in prayer and always have each other's best interest. When there is a solid structure in the family, traditions are kept, and relationships last forever, even through difficulties and sad occasions. A strong family foundation cannot be easily broken. With all of that being said, all foundations need to have Christ as the solid foundation, for it is He that will get us through all trials, temptations, and troubles. If we make sure He is the firm foundation that gives us great hope, we will make it through every storm that life brings our way.

Signs of a Strong Foundation:
Good communication
Trust
Not being afraid of who you are
Knowing your self-worth
Being prepared

Willingness to start over
Admitting when you are wrong
Putting in effort
Making good decisions

Somebody once said, "If a marriage or friendship has a strong, solid foundation, everything else can be repaired."

About The Author

Beverly Vereen is an author, wife, friend, sister, a woman that loves God, and the mother of four beautiful children, one son and three daughters. I have a passion to help and motivate others.

Made in the USA
Columbia, SC
30 June 2022